CHEAPER THAN THERAPY

Running Press
Hachette Book Group
1290 Avenue of the Americas, New York, NY 10104
www.runningpress.com
@Running_Press

Printed in China

First Edition: June 2016

Published by Running Press, an imprint of Perseus Books, LLC, a subsidiary of Hachette Book Group, Inc. The Running Press name and logo is a trademark of the Hachette Book Group.

The Hachette Speakers Bureau provides a wide range of authors for speaking events.
To find out more, go to www.hachettespeakersbureau.com or call (866) 376-6591.

The publisher is not responsible for websites (or their content) that are not owned by the publisher.

Cover illustration by Mario Zucca
Cover design by Sarah Pierson and Ashley Prine
Interior design by Ashley Prine

IMAGE CREDITS
Decorative elements throughout and frame on p. 6 courtesy of the Library of Congress
p. 6 couch © Clipart.com
pp. 28 and 112 © Dover
p. 39 © belopoppa/Shutterstock
p. 62 and 125 © Morphart Creation/Shutterstock
p. 77 © VladisChern/Shutterstock
p. 89 © Randall Reed/Shutterstock
p. 99 © Hein Nouwens/Shutterstock
p. 137 © chronicler/Shutterstock

Library of Congress Control Number: 2015954074

ISBN: 978-0-7624-5976-6 (paperback)

RRD-S

11   10   9   8   7   6   5   4   3

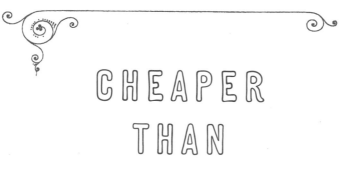

CHEAPER THAN THERAPY

– A GUIDED JOURNAL –

RUNNING PRESS

PHILADELPHIA

TELL ME ABOUT IT

Everybody needs a place to spill their guts from time to time so they can deal with their messy minds and get their heads on straight. But who needs to pay a therapist to ask, "How does that make you feel?" when this awesome, little book does exactly that for just pennies a page?! After all, therapy is just a place to dump out all your feelings and tell the stories that you're too embarrassed to tell your friends. And now, fortunately, you don't have to pay hundreds of dollars for someone to feign interest in your inner turmoil. By following the simple prompts and exercises contained in this totally reputable* journal, you can unload all your baggage into one neat and attractive package, without taking any of it super seriously.

You can talk about your dad, your job, your love life (or lack thereof), your dreams, how your cat is plotting to kill you (it totally is), and whatever else your reality-addled mind wants to spit up. Because let's face it: The world is tough, families are nuts, friends are annoying, and your boss is an asshole. You've got to get it out somewhere, and now you don't have to pay tons of money to get it out on someone else's couch where loads of other people have already spilled their dirty, gutsy secrets (which is pretty gross when you think about it). And the best part is, you can do it all without taking any of your own bullshit too much to heart. I believe Freud said, Maslow agreed, and Pavlov wrote a dissertation stating that laughter is qualitatively and quantifiably the best medicine. So go ahead and unleash your inner demons—and then laugh in their stupid faces!

*Reputability may vary with personal standards.

How do you feel today?

_____
_____
_____
_____
_____
_____
_____
_____
_____
_____

Tell me more about that.

_____
_____
_____
_____
_____
_____
_____
_____

WHAT IS YOUR EARLIEST MEMORY?

DID SOMETHING NEGATIVE HAPPEN TO YOU THIS WEEK?

How would you have liked to handle that instead?

WHAT IS/WAS YOUR FATHER LIKE?

LET'S EXPLORE THAT FURTHER.

TELL ME ABOUT YOUR RECURRING DREAM.

WHAT DO *YOU* THINK THAT MEANS?

WHAT IS YOUR MOST UNCOMFORTABLE MEMORY?

WHY DO YOU THINK YOU CAN'T GET PAST IT?

RORSCHACH TEST

Inkblot, or Rorschach, tests have been around since the 1920s. They're used as a method of analyzing the way people perceive the world by using abstract images and asking the testees to describe them. In this case, you are the testee, and I shouldn't say any more lest I influence your reaction. I hope your pen is ready!

Study this image.

WHAT DO YOU SEE?

☐ A butt

☐ Boobs

☐ A crab

☐ Lady down-under parts

☐ An ink splatter

☐ Pure evil

☐ Medium evil

☐ Evil light

☐ Fireworks

☐ Your father

☐ Some sort of terrifying insect that's probably under your skin right now, laying eggs that will hatch and eat your brain from the inside out

See the reverse side of this page for some serious analysis.

WHAT DID YOU SEE IN THE INK?

A butt.
You like big butts, and you should stop lying about it.

Boobs.
Your mother didn't breastfeed you for long enough, so now you see boobs everywhere. There are worse fates.

A crab.
Totally!! That's what you'd see if you were sane. The rest of these answers? Yikes.

Lady down-under parts.
You're a bit of a perv, but not in a terrible way. Friendly suggestion: Watch less porn.

An ink splatter.
You're no fun, and people don't invite you to parties. Pretend to have an imagination.

Pure evil.
You poor, poor person.

Medium evil.

You're wishy-washy and you watch the news too much.

Evil light.

You're a realist who knows everything is a little bit evil. Keep up the suspicious work!

Fireworks.

You're an optimist who listens to too much Katy Perry.

Your father.

You may want to pay for a real therapist . . .

Some sort of terrifying insect that's probably under your skin right now, laying eggs that will hatch and eat your brain from the inside out. Why are you still reading this book? Get some tweezers and go to work, NOW! Just kidding. You're nuts, but you should be able to self medicate with some Dr. Phil and herbal teas.

TELL ME ABOUT A TIME YOU FEEL LIKE YOUR VOICE WASN'T HEARD.

HOW DO YOU THINK YOU COULD HAVE BEEN MORE FORCEFUL IN THAT SITUATION?

LET'S EXPLORE A MEMORY YOU FREQUENTLY REVISIT.

WHAT DO YOU THINK THAT SAYS ABOUT YOU?

WHAT IS YOUR BIGGEST REGRET?

<u>How do you think you can overcome it?</u>

WHAT WAS YOUR CHILDHOOD BULLY LIKE?

IF THAT PERSON WERE HERE RIGHT NOW, WHAT WOULD YOU SAY TO HIM/HER?

HOW WELL DO YOU GET ALONG WITH YOUR MOTHER?

_____

_____

_____

_____

_____

_____

_____

_____

_____

_____

WHAT SHOULD SHE HAVE DONE DIFFERENTLY?

_____

_____

_____

_____

_____

_____

_____

_____

ARE YOU SEEING ANYONE?

WHAT IS HE/SHE LIKE? IF NOT, WHAT WOULD YOU LIKE

HIM/HER TO BE LIKE?

How satisfied are you in your work?

_____

_____

_____

_____

_____

_____

_____

_____

_____

_____

Oh, really? What would you rather be doing?

_____

_____

_____

_____

_____

_____

_____

_____

WORD ASSOCIATION TEST

For each given word, write down the first word that comes into your head. Don't cheat! If you do, you're only cheating yourself, cheater. Then flip to the next page for your totally real results.

Banana _____

Popsicle _____

House _____

Green _____

Box _____

Wild _____

Father _____

Needle _____

Pencil   _____

Sad   _____

Friendly   _____

Cold   _____

Cow   _____

Fork   _____

Anxiety   _____

Kiss   _____

Die   _____

Women   _____

Lamp   _____

If you usually said a word that was the opposite of the given word . . .

Example: Up / Down

You're a contradictory type of person who loves to get a rise out of people and be difficult. Most likely a middle child. You have no idea how to get attention in a good way. The technical term for this is "jerk." Try agreeing with people for once in your whole damn life and see how that goes.

If you usually said a word that was the definition of the given word . . .

Example: Bread / Wheat

A smart guy, huh? You just think you know everything. What bread is made out of. Which way is north. How many miles to the moon. Well, no one likes a know-it-all, so just stop it! Pretend you're slightly less insufferable at least some of the time. Unless someone asks you for directions. Then you're a delight!

If you usually said a word that was a synonym of the given word . . .

Example: Ocean / Sea

Yawn! Why are you still here when you should be out getting a personality? Your literal mind with its one-to-one associations is sooo predictable, how do people even stand you? Hm, they probably don't. Try being interesting, and maybe people will stop falling asleep when you talk to them.

If you usually said a word that was a judgment of the given word . . .

Example: Hairdo / Butt-Ugly

Oh, like your hair is so cool! You are what's known in the therapeutic community as a Judgy McJudgerson; someone filled with opinions that feel to you like facts. Newsflash! They're not. So follow the old adage: If you can't say anything nice, don't say anything at all. Unless you're funny about it.

If you usually said a word that was a repeat of the given word . . .

Example: Mountain / Mountain

Seriously? Jeez. Well, you're dull as dishwater, but at least you're on the level. Nope, no crazy here. Just lots of humdrum bleakness that hardly makes life worth living. Staying the course. Steady as she goes. Business as usual. Lots of other played-out clichés that represent your personality.

TELL ME ABOUT YOUR CIRCLE OF FRIENDS.

ARE YOU THE MOST ATTRACTIVE?

WHEN YOU WERE LITTLE, WHAT DID YOU WANT TO BE WHEN YOU GREW UP?

WHEN DID YOU GIVE UP ON THAT DREAM?

WHAT HAS BEEN THE HARDEST LIFE LESSON YOU'VE EVER LEARNED?

WOW, THAT SOUNDS TERRIBLE! HOW DID YOU LEARN IT?

LOOK INTO MY LINED PAGES. DEEPER, DEEPER. YOU'RE GETTING SLEEPY, SLEEPIER. NOW TELL ME YOUR DIRTIEST SECRET.

_____

_____

_____

_____

_____

_____

_____

_____

EW! I MEAN, GO ON . . .

_____

_____

_____

_____

_____

_____

_____

_____

WHAT QUALITIES DO YOU LOOK FOR IN A BFF?

_____

_____

_____

_____

_____

_____

_____

_____

_____

_____

DO YOU REALLY THINK YOU POSSESS THOSE QUALITIES?

_____

_____

_____

_____

_____

_____

_____

_____

WHAT IS THE WORST NIGHTMARE YOU CAN REMEMBER?

_____

_____

_____

_____

_____

_____

_____

_____

_____

WHAT DO YOU THINK IT MEANS?

_____

_____

_____

_____

_____

_____

_____

WHAT DID YOU ACTUALLY WANT TO DO WITH YOUR LIFE?

_____

_____

_____

_____

_____

_____

_____

_____

_____

WHAT'S KEEPING YOU FROM DOING IT?

_____

_____

_____

_____

_____

_____

_____

_____

WHAT WOULD JUNG SAY?

Carl Jung (pronounced "young") is the famous psychiatrist who invented analytical psychology. He said a ton of stuff, and his more fun theories centered on the collective unconscious and dreams. Let's not get into too much technical mumbo-jumbo; suffice it to say, there are some prevailing symbols in your dreams that determine what kind of crazy you are. So let's get into that head of yours!

Write down a recent vivid dream here, then flip the page to get Junged.

_____

_____

_____

_____

_____

_____

_____

_____

_____

_____

GET JUNGED!

Jung identified seven archetypes of symbols that mean the same thing, no matter who's dreaming them. Apparently because we're all one and psychically linked and other hippie-type stuff. So what was in your dream?

1. The Persona
This is when you dream about yourself. You may show up as a bird or a dung beetle, but you still know it's you. And that you you see is the you you think you present to the world. So if you're terrible and failing in your dreams, well, you think people think you're terrible and failing in life. Woof. That sounds awful! And confusing.

2. The Shadow
Is something chasing you, bullying you, stalking you, trying to kill you? Well, bad news, buddy, that shadow is you! It's the weak, angry, scared you who you try to hide from the world. OK, not *bad* news per se, because that you is often giving you a message about something you just need to accept about yourself. Learn to live with yourself, and you'll stop chasing your own tail!

3. The Trickster
Oh, man, this guy's a riot! He shows up doing funny stuff, and making you laugh. Or he shows up and makes you feel totally uncomfortable and embarrassed, making fun of you in front of everyone, particularly after you just embarrassed yourself in real life. Gee, I wonder which is more common?

4. The Anima / Animus

Are you dreaming of a super sexy lady or a big ol' brute? The woman is the anima and the dude is the animus. And, you guessed it, they're both you! (Maybe Jung should have just said there's one dream arche-type, and it's you?) Anyway, these highly characterized ladies and gents represent the feminine and masculine aspects in us all. If you're doing some gender-role reversals in your dreams (ladies growing beards, dudes with boobs), then you may be repressing yourself. Embrace the other side!

5. The Divine Child

Babies or young children showing up? Guess what? This is you, too! In your cute and cuddly, innocent kid form, full of potential and wonder. But kids are annoying, so let's move on.

6. The Wise Old Woman or Man

Apparently this is you telling you what you need to do, but taking on the guise of a teacher or respectable authority figure you'll actually listen to. 'Cause we all know you're not listening to yourself, or you wouldn't have eaten that second sleeve of Girl Scout cookies!

7. The Great Mother

If your mom, grandma, or other nurturing type shows up, she's either there to give you positive reassurance or be a witchy old hag full of death and jealousy. So like a woman, am I right? Or at least dudely interpretations of women dating back to the turn of the century when ladies couldn't be trusted to vote. Ugh. Next!

DIAGNOSIS?

We're mean to ourselves even when we're asleep.

IMAGINE YOUR IDEAL FUTURE. TELL ME ALL ABOUT IT.

HOW DID YOU GET TO THIS PERFECT TOMORROWLAND?

TELL ME ABOUT YOU AS A CHILD.

_____

_____

_____

_____

_____

_____

_____

_____

_____

_____

DO YOU LIKE THAT KID? WHY OR WHY NOT?

_____

_____

_____

_____

_____

_____

_____

_____

IF YOU COULD TELL THAT KID ANYTHING, WHAT WOULD IT BE?

WHAT'S YOUR SEXUAL FANTASY?

OK, NOW TELL ME THE REAL ONE!

WHAT DO YOU THINK THIS FANTASY MEANS?

WHAT DO YOU DO IN YOUR FREE TIME?

OK, NOW HONESTLY, WHAT DO YOU REALLY SPEND MOST OF YOUR

FREE TIME DOING?

IF YOU HAD A MILLION DOLLARS, WHAT'S THE FIRST THING YOU WOULD DO?

NICE! WHAT ELSE WOULD YOU DO?

THE NEEDS TEST

In the 1940s, famed psychologist Abraham Maslow came up with a hierarchy of needs. Needs you need met before you can be a happy, functioning person who walks around with shiny shoes and nicely creased pants. This gleeful, shiny, wrinkle-free state of being is technically known as self-actualized. These needs are as follows:

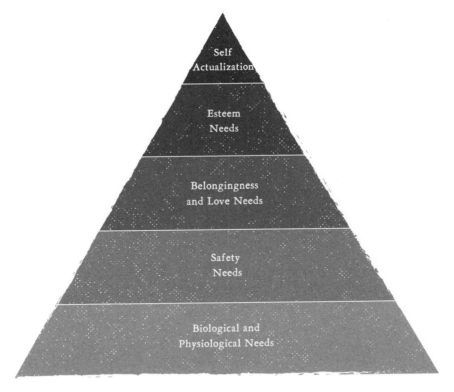

This test is designed to see how far up the pyramid you've climbed. In just a few quick Qs, you'll know if you're limping around at the bottom, or gloriously sunning yourself at the top.

1. Are you hungry?   yes ☐   no ☐

2. Are you sleepy?   yes ☐   no ☐

3. Are you homeless?   yes ☐   no ☐

4. Are your doors unlocked?   yes ☐   no ☐

5. Are you broke?   yes ☐   no ☐

6. Are you pretty sure you have a rare disease?   yes ☐   no ☐

7. Are you single?   yes ☐   no ☐

8. Are you estranged from your family?   yes ☐   no ☐

9. Are you pretty much friendless and alone?   yes ☐   no ☐

10. Do you feel terrible about yourself?   yes ☐   no ☐

11. Are you terrible at everything you do?   yes ☐   no ☐

12. Is everyone aware of how terrible you are?   yes ☐   no ☐

13. Are you falling woefully short of your potential?   yes ☐   no ☐

14. Are your shoes scuffed?   yes ☐   no ☐

15. Are your pants wrinkly?   yes ☐   no ☐

Time to count up your yeses and your nos.

yes ——————

no ——————

JUST HOW NEEDY ARE YOU?

0–3 Yeses

Self Actualization

You are just sitting pretty on the top of the pyramid, basking in the sun and feeling awesome about it! You're self-actualized to the max, and you know it. Yup, life couldn't be better. Just don't start buying into those clichés like, "It's a long fall from the top" or "pride goeth before the fall." Who says "goeth" these days anyway? Not you, you exemplary specimen of mental health and well-being!

4–6 Yeses

Esteem Needs

Hey, you're doing pretty good. You've got your basic needs met. People like you. So why the hell don't you feel better about yourself, you fricken idiot?! Don't you know how many people lower down on the pyramid would *kill* to be at your level, and you're just sitting there thinking that just because you've got a zit and gained five pounds that you've lost all worth as a human being?! Well buck up and climb that last step already!

7–9 Yeses

Belongingness and Love Needs

Feeling a little unloved, huh, buddy? Maybe you got picked last for sports as a kid and that feeling has just carried right on over into adulthood, screwing you up and holding you back. Well, I got news for you. Somebody does love you! No, it's not me. You know who it is. OK, yes, sure, your mom loves you, but that's not who I'm talking about, and you know it! Stop being difficult about this, would you? Jeez, no wonder you're stuck at this level of the pyramid.

10–12 Yeses
Safety Needs
Boo! Scared you, didn't I? That's because you don't feel safe from anything, really. You're scared about money, health, love, and cat burglars with black wool hats and bandit masks over their eyes, and it's really keeping you down. How are you ever going to be happy if you're constantly looking over your shoulder for the bad guy and around the corner for the next disaster? Answer is, you won't. So toughen up already!

13–15 Yeses
Biological and Physiological Needs
Well, this is just rotten. Your most basic needs aren't being met, and you'll never be able to feel good about anything unless you can at least take care of yourself to a minimal degree. Wild animals can even accomplish this step on the pyramid, so you should at least be able to make a go of it. Start eating better. Maybe do a jumping jack or two. Sleep right. You know, all those things those posters in the doctor's office say to do, which hey, maybe you should go visit once in a while!

Why did your last relationship end?

WHAT WOULD YOU HAVE DONE DIFFERENTLY?

TALK ABOUT THE LAST TIME SOMEONE MADE YOU FEEL REALLY AWFUL.

WHAT DID YOU DO IN RESPONSE?

WHAT'S THE EARLIEST MEMORY YOU HAVE OF ABANDONMENT?

HOW DO YOU THINK THAT AFFECTS YOU TODAY?

TELL ME ABOUT YOUR FIRST SEXUAL ENCOUNTER.

OH. WOW. HOW DID THAT MAKE YOU FEEL?

WHAT ARE YOUR SIBLINGS LIKE (OR FRIENDS YOU CONSIDER SIBLINGS BECAUSE YOUR PARENTS THOUGHT, *ONE IS ENOUGH!*)?

_____

_____

_____

_____

_____

_____

_____

_____

DO YOU THINK THEY ARE MORE OR LESS CRAZY THAN YOU? WHY?

_____

_____

_____

_____

_____

_____

_____

_____

WHAT'S YOUR WORST QUALITY?

DO YOU BLAME YOUR MOTHER OR YOUR FATHER?

ACTUALIZE YOUR BAD SELF

Self-actualization is the process of becoming a truer, better—or at least less awful—version of you. It's figuring out who you really are beneath all the childhood trauma and bad relationship scars, and giving that you a big old hug. Once in this state of being all that you can be, you will be able to march as an army of one, eat lots of breakfasts of champions, and maximize your talents to achieve your wildest hopes and dreams.

The key to finding this "real" you is having the unconditional positive encouragement, empathy, and support from a therapist who is honest, open, and sympathetic. Good thing you have this awesome book to do all that for you! On the next few pages, you'll find all the tools and sustenance you need to blossom into the gorgeous, happy flower that lives inside your brain, the *Selfinium awesomatae*.

Step 1. You need a therapist. That's this book. Well done!

Step 2. Think about who you are, and write down your most prominent personality traits.

_____

_____

_____

_____

_____

_____

Smells a little like BS to me. If you said you're kind, think about all the times you were a huge jerk. Now, what *really* are your most prominent personality traits?

_____

_____

_____

_____

_____

_____

Step 3. I bet that sucked, but exploring the jerk you really are is an important part of blossoming. Go ahead and write down a few of those negative feelings that popped up when you discovered the depths of your own jerkitude.

_____

_____

_____

_____

_____

_____

_____

Step 4. Now forget all that bullshit! You faced it, and now you're totally past it. In fact, you're halfway to actualization, so describe how you're awesome.

_____

_____

_____

_____

_____

_____

_____

Step 5. Good, good. That was an excellent story, and you're an excellent person. Attractive, smart, a real go-getter. Yeah! Now that you're perfectly amazing, what do you want to do with your life?

_____

_____

_____

_____

_____

_____

Step 6. Awesome! You're a genius! You're just about totally cured of any faults and insecurities forever now. All you need to do is write down what you're going to do tomorrow to get one step closer to the life you described above. Now repeat every day for the rest of your life no matter how tired you are or how badly you fail.

_____

_____

_____

_____

_____

WHAT'S YOUR WORST QUALITY?

HOW DO YOU THINK YOU BECAME THAT WAY?

Do you blame your parents? Why?

WOULD YOU DESCRIBE YOURSELF AS HAVING TRUST ISSUES?

OF COURSE YOU DO! WE ALL HAVE THEM. WHERE DO YOU THINK YOURS CAME FROM?

DO YOU EVER HAVE, LET'S SAY, UNSETTLING FANTASIES?

TELL ME MORE ABOUT THAT.

IF YOU COULD BE ANY ANIMAL, WHAT ANIMAL WOULD YOU BE AND WHY?

WHAT IS YOUR BIGGEST FEAR?

THAT SOUNDS TERRIFYING! TELL ME MORE.

TELL ME ABOUT A RECURRING NIGHTMARE.

HOW DOES IT MAKE YOU FEEL WHEN YOU WAKE UP?

THE WHOMP-WHOMP TEST

Feeling down? Got the blues? A lump in your throat? Are you down in the dumps? How about down in the mouth? Maybe you're out of sorts, not a happy camper, stuck in the doldrums. Whatever cliché you want to use to say it, you're sad. But you can get a handle on your heartsickness with this test that's sure to make you feel, well, probably no different, but at least it will distract you for a few minutes! Plus, it will give you a label to put on your particular brand of sad, as in, "Oh, yeah, Larry's just like that. He has acute tublodial buttnoidosis." See, you're feeling better already!

I'm going to give you a series of statements grouped in fours. For every quartet, pick the statement that you identify with most closely in the innards of your tortured heart. Let's begin!

0 I'm feeling pretty damn fine!
1 Meh, I'm OK.
2 Ugh, don't even.
3 What was that? I can't hear you over the sound of my tears.

0 The future is a bright and sunny promise of golden good times.
1 Is it supposed to rain tomorrow?
2 It's probably going to rain tomorrow because I took off from work.
3 Tomorrow will be a torrential suckfest just like all the other torrential suckfests before it.

0 Have I ever mentioned how awesome I am?

1 I'm a pretty OK person. Thanks for asking.

2 I wouldn't blame you if you didn't want to be my friend.
   Whatever. It's fine.

3 Ugh, I'm worse than Putin.

0 Life just keeps rewarding the heck out of my awesomeness!

1 I get a karmic kick in the pants once in a while, but I deserve it.

2 I expect that life has quite a few more deuces to drop on me.

3 Life is a series of unfair, punishing events that lack rhyme, reason,
   or common decency.

0 People are the best!!! LOVE!!

1 People are pretty OK. Usually.

2 Ugh, people.

3 People are the worst!!! HATE!!

0 I feel pretty dang good about the things I've done.

1 Sometimes I feel a little bad about a few things I've done.
   Sorry, world!

2 Oh, wow, yeah. I should not have done a lot of that. Yikes.

3 You really don't want to know about all the terrible stuff I've
   done. Gotta go!

LET'S ADD IT UP!

OK, well done, friend. You've taken the self-indulgent, I mean totally scientific and psychologically important, Whomp-Whomp test. Now let's see how you did!

I scored 0–5! I have euphorisis!

Really? Well, the good news is you are the opposite of sad. You have a condition known as euphorisis, which means everyone can't believe how gosh darn happy you are all the gosh darn time, gosh darn it! Maybe sometimes you're *too* happy. Manic even. You personify the phrase "ignorance is bliss" while grating on the normal people around you with your unwarranted cheerfulness. You're kind of the worst in fact. Ugh, I can't even look at you!

I scored 6–12. I have normania.

Oh hey, what's up, Norm Chomsky? I say that because you are so totally normal. Yup, you got this feeling-sad-when-it's-right-to-feel-sad and feeling-happy-when-it's-right-to-feel-happy thing down pat. Your condition, known as normania, is characterized by being a totally well adjusted human being that is capable of processing emotions like a champ and interacting with other human beings as if they weren't all batshit insane, which, let's face it, they absolutely are. Why did you even buy this book!?

I scored 13–19. I have **debbydownerism.**

Your debbydownerism makes you a glass-half-empty sort of person. You're not really sad in a profound, terminal sense. You just sort of feel like the world is not entirely awesome, you're not entirely awesome, no one is entirely awesome, and nothing will ever be entirely awesome, and that's just how things are. "Meh." That's you all over. The good news is that this is a super-mild condition, but it is contagious and can easily backslide into more serious conditions like negativenancitis and dickweedium.

I scored a 20–26. I have **unfufilledaphilia.**

Having unfulfilledaphilia means that you're pretty sure this crappy world is crapping on you all the time, and there's no way out of the crap heap. But here's another way to look at it: This crappy world craps on us all equally! It's what you do with the crap that matters. You can let it rain down on you until you drown in it. Or you can say, "No more, crap gods!" and pretend it's all chocolate ice cream instead.

WHAT IS YOUR HAPPIEST MEMORY?

WHAT IS YOUR UNHAPPIEST MEMORY?

IF YOU HAD TO PICK ONE ADJECTIVE TO DESCRIBE YOURSELF, WHAT WOULD IT BE AND WHY?

ARE YOU HAPPY WITH THAT AS YOUR PRIMARY SELF-DEFINING CHARACTER TRAIT?

WHAT ADJECTIVES DO YOU THINK OTHERS WOULD USE TO
DESCRIBE YOU? WHY?

DESCRIBE A PROBLEM IN YOUR LIFE THAT YOU SEE AS UNSOLVABLE.

IMAGINE A FRIEND DESCRIBED THAT SAME PROBLEM TO YOU. IS IT

STILL UNSOLVABLE? WHAT ADVICE WOULD YOU GIVE THEM?

IF YOU COULD MAGICALLY MAKE A CHANGE IN YOUR LIFE, WHAT WOULD IT BE?

HOW DO YOU THINK YOU COULD MAKE THAT CHANGE, NON-MAGICALLY?

DO YOU EVER IMAGINE ARGUMENTS WITH OTHERS IN YOUR HEAD? DESCRIBE ONE.

DO YOU THINK IT WOULD ACTUALLY BE BENEFICIAL TO REALIZE THAT FANTASY?

ART THERAPY

Break out your crayons and fruit-scented markers, it's time to heal your psyche through arts and crafts!

Think of the last thing that upset you, then draw it with reckless abandon. Really draw those feelings!

Think about your parents. Draw that feeling hard! Like you're five years old, it's dinner, and they're forcing you to eat cold French-cut string beans from a can. Go, van Gogh!

This is your heart. Fill it up with all the stuff you care about. Try to keep the proportions roughly correct. Don't worry too much about that though—as long as it's perfect, it'll be great!

This is your brain. Draw all the stuff that's jammed in that gray matter. Work, family, deep thoughts, shallow thoughts, did you leave the oven on, and so on . . .

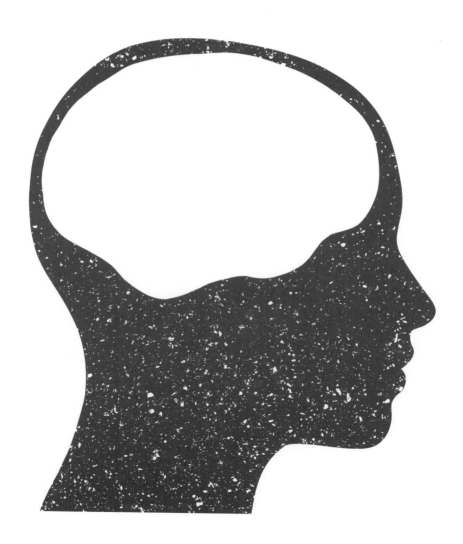

DESCRIBE SOMEONE IN YOUR LIFE WHO REALLY BOTHERS YOU.

IF YOU COULD SAY ANYTHING TO THAT PERSON, CONSEQUENCE FREE, WHAT WOULD IT BE?

WRITE ABOUT A TIME IN YOUR LIFE WHEN YOU WERE TAKEN ADVANTAGE OF.

_____

_____

_____

_____

_____

_____

_____

_____

_____

COULD YOU HAVE DONE ANYTHING TO PREVENT IT?

_____

_____

_____

_____

_____

_____

_____

_____

WHAT CAN YOU DO TO MAKE SURE YOU WON'T BE TAKEN ADVANTAGE
OF IN THAT WAY AGAIN?

WHAT IS SOMETHING YOU'RE REALLY AFRAID OF?

DO YOU THINK THAT'S A REALISTIC FEAR?

_____

_____

_____

_____

_____

_____

_____

_____

_____

HOW DO YOU THINK YOU COULD GET OVER IT?

_____

_____

_____

_____

_____

_____

_____

_____

DESCRIBE A CRINGE-WORTHY EVENT IN YOUR LIFE.

IMAGINE IT HAPPENED TO SOMEONE YOU RESPECT INSTEAD OF TO

YOURSELF. DOES IT STILL SEEM THAT BAD? WHAT WOULD YOU SAY

TO THEM?

IF YOU COULD HAVE ANY SUPERPOWER, WHAT WOULD IT BE?

WHAT IS THE FIRST THING YOU WOULD DO WITH IT?

HOW PSYCHOSEXUAL ARE YOU?

Sigmund Freud, the grandmaster of all things psycho and sexual, proposed that most of your personality becomes fixed by the time you are five. No pressure, kids. As you were moving through the stages of your little life, you were either having your id stroked the right way, allowing your super ego to blossom and your regular ego to thrive, or you were shamed into emotional immaturity and are pretty much like Quasimodo on the inside. You know, either way.

This quiz will help you figure out if you passed a super-important test you didn't even know you were taking, which, as it turns out, defines pretty much your whole life. Let's get into it!

1. Do you ever pee yourself a little?   yes ☐   no ☐

2. Do you smoke?   yes ☐   no ☐

3. Is your sex life kind of the worst?   yes ☐   no ☐

4. Do you relentlessly chew gum?   yes ☐   no ☐

5. Are you confident the opposite sex is superior to yours?
yes ☐   no ☐

6. Do you hate toilet paper?   yes ☐   no ☐

7. Do you get "stage fright" in a public restroom if someone else is
in there?   yes ☐   no ☐

8. Have you sharted in the last year? yes ☐ no ☐

9. Do you bite your nails? yes ☐ no ☐

10. Do you prefer your parent who is the opposite sex (or same sex if you are gay)? Like *really* prefer them? yes ☐ no ☐

11. Are you absolutely cooler than your parent who is the same sex (or opposite sex, if you are gay)? yes ☐ no ☐

12. Were you not at all creeped out by *parent* and *sex* appearing in the same sentences? yes ☐ no ☐

13. Are you lost without a breath mint to suck on? yes ☐ no ☐

14. Are you crazy embarrassed if anyone hears you fart? yes ☐ no ☐

15. Are you utterly without a sex life? yes ☐ no ☐

Let's see how utterly screwed you are! Count up them nos and yeses.

yes _____

no _____

JUST HOW PSYCHOSEXUAL ARE YOU?

0 Yeses: Superior Super-Ego

Congratulations on being about as OK as a human being can hope to be in this world. Not only did your parents feed you, but they potty trained you without shaming you about that terrible business coming out of you. You also didn't get creepily attached to one and competitive with the other in a whole miasma of ick. Nope, you grew up, went to school, made friends, went through puberty, got some (and probably even continue to get some), all without ever yelling out, "Oh, daddy/mommy!" at a really weird time.

1–3 Yeses: Stuck on the Wingdangdoodle Stage

Oh, so close! You made it through most of your childhood OK, but it looks like when you got to the "genital stage" where you have to interact with someone you like—and by like, I mean *like like*, and by interact, I'm stressing the *inter*—you kind of blew it. It was awkward, you didn't know what to do, and you ended up feeling hugely stupid. More than once. Pretty much every time. According to Freud, you've got a long way to go to get past this embarrassment.

4–6 Yeses: Laid Up in Latency

Well, you screwed up in the easiest stage to get through. (Slow, sarcastic clapping.) When you were supposed to be in the sexually latent stage—you know, going to school, making friends, learning about colors—you were thinking waaaaaay too much about the difference between boys and girls, and I'm not talking emotional maturity here. You got fixated on the underwear bits, and that's where you've stayed.

7–9 Yeses: A Phallic Fallacy

Looks like you got caught up in the phallic stage. Back when you were just little, you discovered you had some feel-good parts, and you went NUTS for them! Sadly, that's not the problem. The drama to overcome in this stage is the Oedipus/Electra Complex in which you get too attached to mommy or daddy, and wish the other parent would fall into a hole full of poisonous Gila monsters. A little jealousy would have been alright, but you took it too far, never to be seen as normal again.

10–11 Yeses: Abnormally Anal

Let's just start by saying it's not your fault. It's not your fault that you are either really uptight or really a big, giant mess. Both of those flaws can be totally blamed on your parents. They just didn't potty train you correctly. Can you believe it? All your life's problems come down to that. Weird, huh? Your parents were either too strict or not strict enough, but either way, they shamed the crap out of you for any accidents you had, and that's why you're sad and have no friends.

12–15 Yeses: Orally Obfuscated

From the time you were a mere babe, you were laying down foundations of doom. There you were, a little bundle of joy, happily sucking on bottles and body parts, and all was right with the world. Then weaning came along and ruined everything! You had to start crawling away from the boob to independence, and you hated it. So there you stayed, emotionally trying to reclaim that safe little world where all you had to do was coo, suckle, and poo. Ah, the good ol' days.

DO YOU FEEL WORTHY OF LOVE? WHY OR WHY NOT?

DO YOU FEEL WORTHY OF SCORN? WHY OR WHY NOT?

IF YOU COULD CHANGE ONE THING ABOUT YOUR PAST, WHAT WOULD IT BE?

_____

_____

_____

_____

_____

_____

_____

_____

HOW DO YOU THINK YOU'D BE DIFFERENT NOW IF YOU WERE ABLE TO MAKE THAT CHANGE?

_____

_____

_____

_____

_____

_____

CAN YOU FIND ANY BENEFITS FROM HAVING GONE THROUGH THAT
TOTALLY MISERABLE EXPERIENCE?

WHAT IS THE EARLIEST CHILDHOOD DREAM YOU CAN REMEMBER?

WHAT WAS YOUR FAVORITE GAME TO PLAY AS A CHILD?

Do you think that says anything about your personality today?

DO YOU PREFER GROUP OR SOLO ACTIVITIES? WHY?

DO YOU OFTEN FEEL SMARTER THAN THE PEOPLE AROUND YOU? OR STUPIDER?

DO YOU HAVE ANY EVIDENCE TO BACK THAT UP?

PERSONALITY TEST

What kind of a son-of-a-gun are you, anyway? An introvert? An extrovert? An introverted extrovert with introverted extrovert qualities who is intuitive but judgy? Let's find out! Read the prompts and circle the response that best applies to you.

1. You are a super go-getter.

    Hell yes!   Yup   Meh   Nope   Hell no!

2. You have lots of friends and you hang like whoa.

    Hell yes!   Yup   Meh   Nope   Hell no!

3. You sometimes cry when cute puppies look sad.

    Hell yes!   Yup   Meh   Nope   Hell no!

4. The world is generally a pretty nice place.

    Hell yes!   Yup   Meh   Nope   Hell no!

5. When you have to make a choice, your gut knows what to do.

    Hell yes!   Yup   Meh   Nope   Hell no!

6. After a party, you usually swear you'll never go to another party again.

    Hell yes!   Yup   Meh   Nope   Hell no!

7. Your habits are pretty much set in stone.

     Hell yes!   Yup   Meh   Nope   Hell no!

8. You're always on the lookout for shiny, new things to do.

     Hell yes!   Yup   Meh   Nope   Hell no!

9. Sticking to the rules is the only way to get the gold.

     Hell yes!   Yup   Meh   Nope   Hell no!

10. Reason is stupid. Emotions rule!

     Hell yes!   Yup   Meh   Nope   Hell no!

11. When you get to a crowded room, you dive right into the center.

     Hell yes!   Yup   Meh   Nope   Hell no!

12. You are easily tempted into bad, wicked, naughty behavior.

     Hell yes!   Yup   Meh   Nope   Hell no!

13. You LOVE to talk about your feelings.

     Hell yes!   Yup   Meh   Nope   Hell no!

14. You rarely ponder the why of existence. That junk's for nerds!

     Hell yes!   Yup   Meh   Nope   Hell no!

15. You are excited about life!!!!!!!!

     Hell yes!   Yup   Meh   Nope   Hell no!

WHO ARE YOU?

Break out that calculator, because it's time to add up who you are! Give yourself 5 points for every *Hell yes!*; 4 points for every *Yup*; 3 points for your *Mehs*; 2 points for the *Nopes*; and 1 point each time you said *Hell no!*

0–3 Points
Introverted Judgy Pants with Sensitive Feelings

Oh, so you hate fun. And people. And probably baby hedgehogs, you monster. Who doesn't love baby hedgehogs!? You, that's who! You'd rather sit in the corner, reading some sad book about dysfunctional people who say they're broken but really think they're just better than everyone else. The good news is that in a hostage situation, no one will probably notice you, so you'll likely survive. As if you care.

4–6 Points
Introverted Ponderer with Eyes in the Back of Your Head

You may not be the life of the party, even if it's just you and an elderly cat who showed up to this "party." But that's OK, kind of. You might not be thrilling company, but you do like to absorb the things around you. Take it all in and contemplate what it all means. Which is interesting, if you think about it, which you will. Repeatedly.

7–9 Points

Sensitive Somethingvert Who Doesn't Know Whether They're Coming or Going

You'll likely never get hit by a car, because you are right in the middle of the road. You could go out, you could stay in. You could follow your heart, you could think it through. You could shout from the rooftops, or you could take a nap. You know, whatever. This makes you exceptionally easy to get along with, so you're probably having a really nice, mild time of things. Hooray?

10–12 Points

Enthusiastic Extrovert with Some Semblance of Discretion

You are just out there, living it! But not living it too much. Just enough. Usually. You want to be with people, engaged in what they're doing, basking in their attention as you suck up their life force. But you know whose life force sucks and is therefore not worth sucking up. You intuit things and think them through instead of just going with your gut, which is always screaming, "DEVOUR MORE SOULS!!"

13–15 Points

Extroverted Touchy-Feely Type with No Judgment Skills

The world is a glorious bouncy castle full of rainbows and delights. And you want ALL OF IT! You're outgoing, going out there, and people sometimes think you're out of your gonads because you're just so damn open to everyone and everything. It's exhilarating, but I'd wager dollars to donuts it gets you into the occasional pickle, which is the last thing you want from your donuts. You are who you are, but one small bit of advice: Stop hugging bums.

DESCRIBE THE BEST MEMORY YOU HAVE WITH A PARENT.

DESCRIBE THE WORST MEMORY YOU HAVE WITH A PARENT.

DESCRIBE THE BEST MEMORY YOU HAVE WITH A FRIEND.

ARE YOU STILL FRIENDS WITH THAT PERSON? WHY OR WHY NOT?

WHY DO YOU THINK YOU VALUE THAT MEMORY?

DESCRIBE THE BEST MEMORY YOU HAVE WITH AN ANIMAL.

DO YOU SOMETIMES SUSPECT THAT ANIMALS ARE BETTER THAN HUMANS? WHY OR WHY NOT?

DESCRIBE THE BEST MEMORY YOU HAVE OF DOING SOMETHING ON YOUR OWN.

_____

_____

_____

_____

_____

_____

_____

_____

_____

WOULD YOU STILL DO SOMETHING LIKE THAT TODAY? WHY OR WHY NOT?

_____

_____

_____

_____

_____

_____

_____

_____

DESCRIBE THE WORST MEMORY YOU HAVE OF BEING ALONE.

_____

_____

_____

_____

_____

_____

_____

_____

HOW CAN YOU AVOID HAVING THAT HAPPEN AGAIN? (ALCOHOL, TV, AND INTERNET AIDS EXCLUDED!)

_____

_____

_____

_____

_____

_____

WHO *WERE* YOU?

Sometimes our past traumas can get in the way of our todays. Maybe you had a bad childhood where the TV stood in for your parents, or maybe you had a bad childhood in the seventeenth century and a dirty rag stood in for your parents. Past-life regression therapy will help you figure out who you *were* so you can deal with who you *are*. By answering a few totally scientific questions, we'll find out about this past life of yours and why it's getting all up in your current business.

1. Someone cuts you off in traffic. How does that make you feel?
   a. You don't even notice that small affront in the vast ocean of affronts that is your life.
   b. If you could, you'd challenge that brute to a duel.
   c. You're unfazed as you flutter along on your way.
   d. Your blood drums in your ear as you imagine decimating the opposing car with a battle-ax.
   e. You didn't even notice, since you were in the back of the limo.

2. How do you feel about snakes?
   a. Damn buggers are everywhere, but at least they don't taste terrible.
   b. Gasp! Someone should take care of those dizzy ghouls.
   c. Snakes? No bother; they're beneath me.
   d. Their skins make frightfully good accessories.
   e. It's a love/hate relationship, really.

3. Your boss tells you that you can't take the vacation days you requested.

   a. Doesn't matter. You couldn't really afford a vacation anyway.

   b. Unacceptable! You already have your tickets for your European tour, and you're going.

   c. Life is short! You're going anyway.

   d. You picture yourself climbing over the cubical walls into that nerd's office and laying waste to everything you find.

   e. Unlikely, as you are the boss.

4. What's your dream house like?

   a. If the floor isn't made of dirt, you're psyched!

   b. Ideally, the servants' quarters would be far enough away that you'd never hear a peep from them. And fireplaces, lots of fireplaces.

   c. Something with lots of windows and a greenhouse would be just lovely.

   d. Permanent structures are for suckers. You split your time between the ground and someone else's house.

   e. Big stones, the highest ceilings imaginable, and lots of wall art seems about right.

5. Where do you think you'll be buried?

   a. A ditch somewhere. If I had it to myself—unlikely—that'd be nice.

   b. Oh, with the rest of the family in the old crypt, you suspect.

   c. A pretty garden with lots of flowers and maybe some nice mud.

   d. On the field of battle! Where else?

   e. Ideally with your spouse, somewhere grand yet mysterious.

Time to tally your answer to find out why you're bananas! How many times did you circle:

a ____   b ____   c ____   d ____   e____

If you need a tie-breaker question, answer this question and add 3 to the tally of the corresponding letter above.
What is your favorite food?
  a. Boiled potatoes, please.
  b. Something rich, probably in pie form.
  c. Anything sweet!
  d. Meat, preferably on the bone.
  e. Bread and fish for me.

If you answered mostly *a*, you were probably a mud farmer in the dark ages! OK, that's probably not something to be too excited about. You were part of an abused peasant class that could not read or write, but instead labored pretty much non-stop for some lords that got fat off your hard work mucking around in the mud. Today, you probably feel like whatever woes come your way are par for the course, and all you can do is bear it. Grinning is not recommended.

If you answered mostly *b*, you were probably a Victorian fop! Oh, how stylish and wealthy you were. All those powders and wigs and frills. Everything was rather butter upon bacon, as they used to say. Today, however, you suffer from the overwhelmingly oppressive emotional repression of the olden days. Where you could never say what you meant, but what you did say better sound like poetry! Now you'd rather eat some "bow wow mutton" than talk about your feelings.

If you answered mostly *c*, you were
a pretty butterfly!

How beautiful and carefree you were. Wing-
ing about in the prairie, drinking nectar
from delicate flowers. Or urine and sweat,
because butterflies LOVE that stuff. Today,
you retain that flighty quality, twitting around from one thing to the
next, never staying long because, hey, life is short! Really short. You're
also prone to secluding yourself for long periods of time and coming
out the other side an utterly different person.

If you answered mostly *d*, you were a Mongolian warrior!
The battle drums beat in your head constantly. You want to conquer
and hack at things with an axe and yell and travel and maybe ride
a decked-out elephant. Today, you have a *very* short fuse, and your
instinct is to annihilate your enemies. People probably find that . . .
disconcerting. They also probably wish you'd shower more and clean
the blood out from under your fingernails once in a while.

If you answered mostly *e*, you were Cleopatra!
Sure, everyone thinks they were probably Cleopatra or Napoléon or
someone like that, but, hey, someone had to actually *be* them, and that
person is you! You ruled Egypt, married your brothers, were commem-
orated by Shakespeare, and probably had some cats. Today, your love of
cats persists, you're pretty dysfunctional when it comes to siblings, and
you feel like you should be in charge of everything you see. That's fair.

DO YOU THINK PEOPLE DISCRIMINATE AGAINST YOU BECAUSE OF YOUR GENDER OR RACE?

WHAT DO YOU WANT TO SAY TO THOSE RACIST GENDERISTS?

DO YOU HAVE SOME OF YOUR OWN GENDER BIASES? OF COURSE YOU DO! WHAT ARE THEY?

WHERE DO YOU THINK YOUR IDEAS ABOUT GENDER COME FROM?

IS THERE SOMETHING YOU WANT TO CHANGE ABOUT YOUR PERCEPTIONS?

TELL ME ABOUT YOUR ARCHNEMESIS AT WORK.
(DON'T LIE, WE ALL HAVE ONE. MAYBE EVEN MANY!)

WHAT DO YOU FANTASIZE ABOUT DOING TO THIS STUPID AND
OBVIOUSLY INFERIOR JERK?

WHAT ARE YOU MOST AFRAID THAT PEOPLE ARE THINKING WHEN THEY MEET YOU?

DOES THAT REALLY SEEM LIKE A REALISTIC FEAR? WHY OR WHY NOT?

_____

_____

_____

_____

_____

_____

_____

_____

_____

_____

WHAT CAN YOU DO TO NOT BE THAT PERSON YOU'RE AFRAID PEOPLE WILL SEE WHEN THEY LOOK AT YOU?

_____

_____

_____

_____

_____

_____

_____

FAMILY THERAPY

Let's face it, families are the root cause of most mental woes. Whether it be nature or nurture, that pack of nut jobs really screwed you up! It's time to get healthy, or at least show those jerks up by trying, with a little family therapy.

To give your inner child a hug and maybe a Happy Meal toy, answer the questions below. Then call up a parent, ask them the questions, and record their answers below.

1. My childhood was:

   a. Pretty lovely and uneventful with lots of toys, hugs, candy, and love.

   b. Spent largely in front of the TV.

   c. A very loud sequence of virtually nonstop tantrums.

   d. So entirely repressed that you don't remember most of it.

Your answer: _____ Your parent's answer: _____

2. Why do you love ___[rival family member]___ more than me?

   a. He/she is smarter.

   b. He/she is better looking.

   c. He/she is far less annoying.

   d. All of the above.

Your answer: _____ Your parent's answer:_____

3. What is the biggest lie you ever told me?

   a. That Sparky is buried upstate when in fact his ashes are in a cabinet in the kitchen.

   b. Santa didn't come that one year because he saw me (as in you, the kid, don't argue with me!) rubbing myself inappropriately against the arm of the couch.

   c. You love all your children equally.

   d. My resemblance to the mailman, while disconcerting, is merely coincidental.

Your answer: _____ Your parent's answer: _____

4. My birth was:

   a. An expected and blessed event.

   b. An unexpected but still blessed event.

   c. An expected event that turned out to be a horrible mistake.

   d. An unexpected event that turned into a horrible mistake.

Your answer: _____ Your parent's answer: _____

5. Are you actually my real mother/father?

   a. Of course! Stop asking that! Wishing won't make you someone else's kid.

   b. Of course not! Let's all be thankful for at least that.

   c. If I could say no, believe me, I would.

   d. Yes, my sweet little progeny whom I adore!

Your answer: _____ Your parent's answer: _____

WHAT'S YOUR FAMILIAL FAMILIARITY?

This quiz wasn't so much about the answers, fascinating though they were, but how well yours matched your parent's. The first step to repairing that umbilical cord so rudely snipped all those years ago is to understand how your parent saw things, and thus better grasp their excuses for messing with your mind. So count up all the matching answers between you and your giver of life.

0 Matching Answers

Are you sure you were talking to *your* parent and not someone else's? Because it really seems like you grew up in different households. You share no memories, no shared vision, and nothing in common. You might as well call it quits and find some other old person who's lonely and needs someone to feel disappointed in.

1 Matching Answer

You probably spent a lot of time at a neighbor's house being raised by their crazy-ass parents. Maybe you should have called one of them to answer these questions. In fact, go do that. I'll wait. No answer, huh? Well, you don't have a lot in common with your own family, but you never really hung out with them anyway, so why start now?

2 Matching Answers

You might not see eye to eye on everything, but at least you have some semblance of the same story. This is a good starting point to healthify-ing your family dynamic. All you have to do is force your parent into re-remembering more of the past the same way you do. Hypnosis might work. Or maybe doctor some old family movies?

3 Matching Answers

This is a good, healthy level of similar-but-not-the-same stories. It's only right that they should remember things a little differently than you do. Any problems you have nowadays stem from you ultimately becoming people who just fundamentally don't like each other.

4 Matching Answers

Everyone's pretty clear on what went down, however, odds are if you took this quiz, no one enjoyed it. At least you're generally on good footing for agreeing on what the problem is: crappy parenting and crappy childing. It was just a big crapfest. Only way to fix it now is to pretend it didn't happen. Repress, repress, repress!

5 Matching Answers

You're all in total agreement about what your childhood was like, and that's weird. You were just a kid! How come you and your parent remember it exactly the same way? That just doesn't feel right. Therapy is all about feelings, after all, and yours are wrong. Maybe you should consider taking a break from your family. See other parents. Call up some friends' families and see what they're doing.

WHAT DO YOU HOPE PEOPLE WILL SEE WHEN THEY LOOK AT YOU?

DO YOU THINK PEOPLE SEE THAT NOW? WHY OR WHY NOT?

WHAT CAN YOU DO TO MAKE SURE PEOPLE SEE THAT WINNER YOU WANT THEM TO SEE?

WHAT DO YOU HAVE TO CUT OUT TO MAKE SURE YOU DON'T COMPROMISE THAT WINNING GO-GETTER OF AN AWESOME YOU?

Do you often get frustrated with the people around you?

_____

_____

_____

_____

_____

_____

_____

_____

What, you think you're better than everyone else or something?

_____

_____

_____

_____

_____

_____

DO YOU OFTEN FEEL LIKE THE PEOPLE AROUND YOU ARE FRUSTRATED WITH YOU? WHY?

HOW DO YOU THINK YOUR PARENTS SCREWED YOU UP?

HOW CAN YOU OVERCOME THAT INEVITABLE DAMAGE THAT ALL PARENTS INFLICT ON THEIR CHILDREN?

HOW DO YOU THINK YOUR SIBLINGS SCREWED YOU UP?

HOW CAN YOU OVERCOME THAT INEVITABLE DAMAGE THAT ALL SIBLINGS INFLICT ON THEIR BROTHERS AND SISTERS?

DESCRIBE YOUR CURRENT STATE OF BLISSFUL, PERFECT MENTAL HEALTH UPON COMPLETING THIS JOURNAL.*

*IF YOU'RE STILL NOT TOTALLY CURED OF EVER HAVING A SINGLE NEGATIVE THOUGHT, PURCHASE ANOTHER COPY OF THIS JOURNAL AND START AGAIN.